Leaders of Religion
MOSES

Dilwyn Hunt M.A.

OLIVER & BOYD

Acknowledgements

The author and publishers wish to thank the following for permission to reproduce copyright photographs in this book:

Page 4, Britain/Israel Public Affairs Committee; page 15, Werner Braun; page 24, Werner Braun; inside back cover, J. Allan Cash Ltd.

Illustrated by Joanna Troughton

Oliver & Boyd
Longman House
Burnt Mill, Harlow
Essex CM20 2JE

A division of Longman Group Ltd

Illustrated by

Tenth impression 1995
ISBN 0 05 003846 X

Set in Palatino and Helvetica. Linotron 202

Produced by Longman Singapore Publishers Pte Ltd
Printed in Singapore

The Publisher's policy is to use paper manufactured from sustainable forests.

CONTENTS

The Books of Moses (the *Torah*)
being carried in procession
during a service in a synagogue.

INTRODUCTION

In a number of world religions certain people are regarded as the great leaders or teachers of that religion. Some of these teachers are called Founders because it was largely through their efforts that a new religion began. Jesus of Nazareth, for example, is often called the Founder of Christianity. Gautama, the Buddha, was the Founder of Buddhism.

In the religion of Islam the title Founder is not used. Nevertheless there are certain people who are regarded as the Messengers of God. The greatest of these is Muhammad.

In Judaism there are many great leaders, including Abraham, Jacob and Joseph. For most Jewish people today the greatest leader of them all is Moses. This book looks at the story of Moses' life. Moses lived long ago and parts of his life are not known to us. It is possible to interpret his life in different ways. Did God really speak to Moses? Were the ten plagues miracles? Did the Red Sea really part in the middle? Were the laws Moses taught from God? The answers to these questions are not clear, and where possible each person must make up his or her own mind.

In this book there are a number of plays, newspaper articles and radio programmes. These are, of course, imaginary. Even the plays should not be thought to be attempts to reconstruct historical events exactly. Their purpose is to introduce readers in a lively and appealing way to one of the world's great religions, Judaism, and the life of a great man, Moses.

UNIT 1

Victims of Slavery

Moses was one of the earliest people we know who was prepared to fight for justice and freedom. He talked about how force should not be used to bully others and how people must be allowed to worship the God they believe in. He also taught that laws can help to protect people from the uncaring, the selfish and the greedy. Because of what he said and did, it is not only the Jewish people who respect and admire Moses, so do Christians, Muslims and large numbers of other people.

In the Bible we are told that Moses' parents were Jewish, so to understand Moses it is important to learn something about the first Jewish people.

3500 years ago the Jewish people were not known by that name but were usually called the Hebrews. They were only a small tribe, perhaps a hundred men and women, and they lived in the area between the Mediterranean Sea and the river Euphrates. Although tiny compared with the surrounding great nations, the Hebrew people felt themselves to be different from other people. They believed in one universal and all-powerful God. This God, they believed, took particular interest in them, looked after and cared for them, and had promised them a land called Canaan as their own.

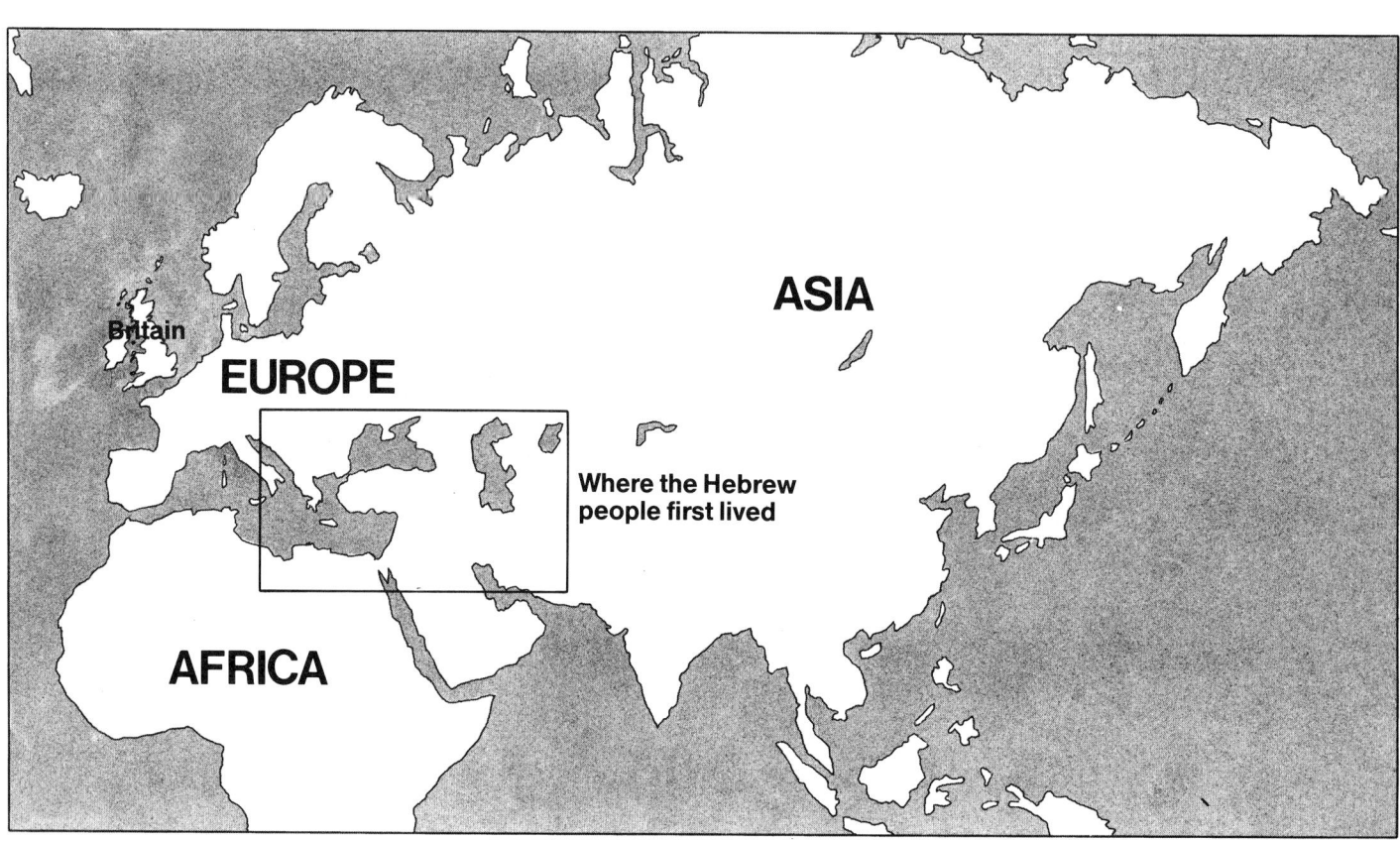

Britain

EUROPE

ASIA

Where the Hebrew people first lived

AFRICA

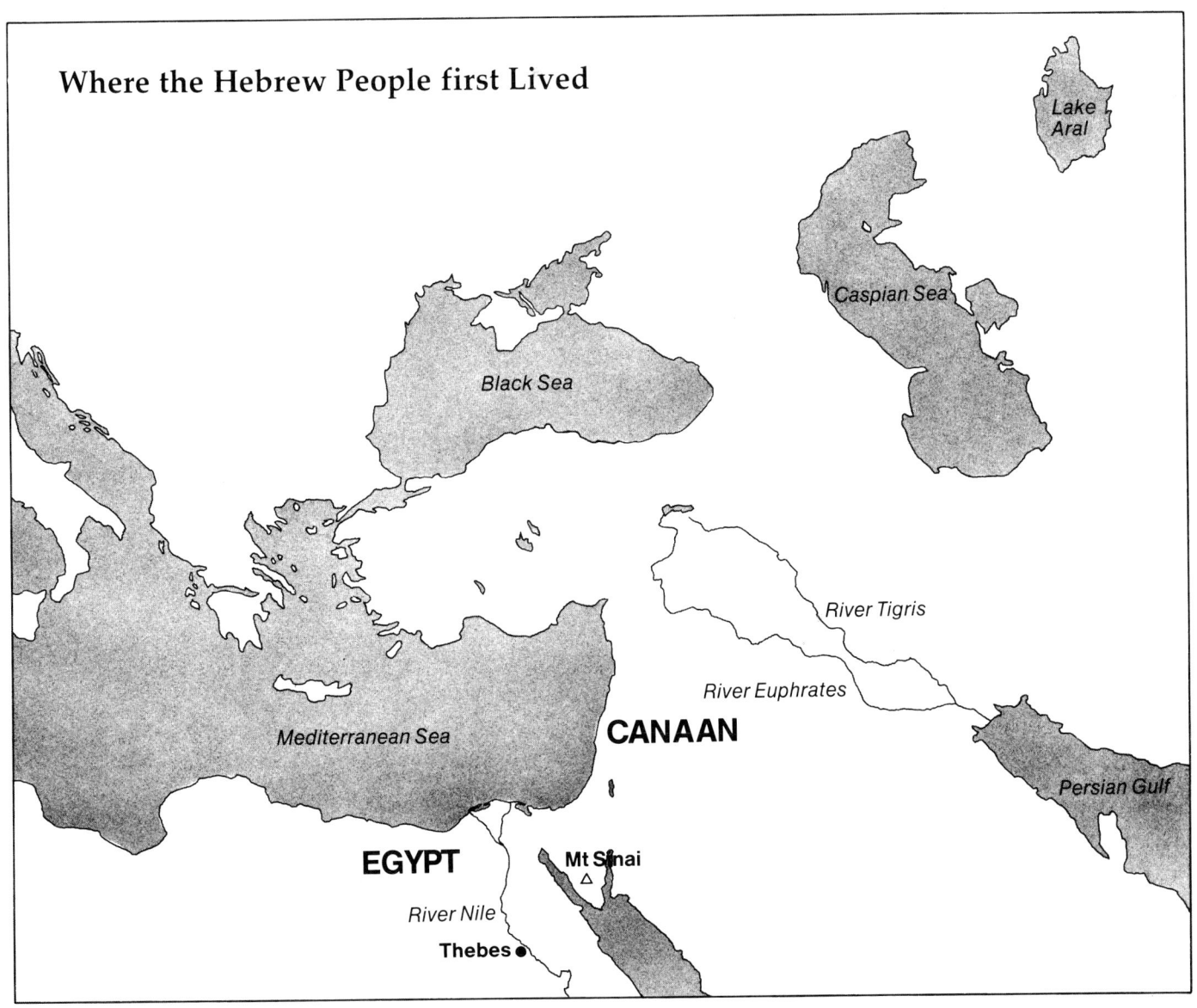

Where the Hebrew People first Lived

In the first book of the Bible (Genesis) we can read about the Hebrew people and their leaders: Abraham, Isaac, Jacob and Joseph. We are told that Joseph led the Hebrew people into Egypt where they were able to live happily in peace. However, over the years some of them forgot about their special God and worshipped instead the same gods as the Egyptians. While this was happening, a new ruler of Egypt came to power and the Hebrew people were forced into slavery and made to work for the Egyptians. As life for the slaves became more and more miserable, even more Hebrew people lost their faith. Many decided that their special God had deserted them.

At this point the Hebrew people seemed crushed. Their freedom had gone, their religion was dying...what could possibly save them? On the brink of disaster the Hebrew people were saved – they gained their freedom, they regained their faith and they found the Promised Land. Jewish people today believe that it was God that achieved all this but that God worked through the man called Moses.

'So they made the people of Israel
serve with rigour, and made their lives
bitter with hard service...'
(Exodus, Chapter 1, verses 13–14.)

The Bible tells us of Moses' extraordinary survival as a baby. About
1250 BCE, the ruler of Egypt, the Pharaoh, decided that there were too
many Hebrew slaves. To reduce their number he cruelly ordered that
all Hebrew boys should be killed. One Hebrew mother, frightened
that her baby boy would die, laid the child in a watertight basket
which she then placed on the river Nile. The basket, with the baby
inside, was discovered by the Pharaoh's daughter. The Bible tells us
that she adopted the baby and called him Moses and he was brought
up as an Egyptian nobleman.

'When she opened it she saw the child;
and lo, the babe was crying.
She took pity on him and said,
"This is one of the Hebrews' children"'
(Exodus, Chapter 2, verse 6.)

Read the story of the birth of Moses in the Bible, Exodus, Chapter 2, verses 1–10.

What have you remembered?

Complete the sentences. Match the phrases in the left-hand column with phrases from the right.

1.	People who believe in Judaism are called	special God
2.	The story of Moses is found in the	the Hebrews
3.	3500 years ago the Jewish people were called	the Egyptians
4.	The Hebrew people believed God had promised them the	Jews
5.	While living in Egypt some of the Hebrews forgot about their	Land of Canaan
6.	The Hebrew people were forced into slavery and were made to work for	Bible

What do you know?

7. Apart from Judaism, name two other religions in which Moses is particularly admired or revered.
8. Name one of the leaders of the Hebrew people before Moses.
9. What was the special name given to the rulers of the Egyptians?
10. What was the job of the Egyptian taskmasters?
11. Moses lived about 1250 BCE. What do the letters BCE stand for?

What do you think?

12. Why do you think some of the Hebrew people lost their faith when they settled in Egypt?
13. Other than Moses, do you know anyone else who fought against slavery? Who was he or she? What did she or he do?
14. Leaders of religion are often greatly admired.
    Can you think of anyone today whom you admire? If so who and why?
15. Great leaders are often said to have 'charisma'.
    Find out and explain what the word 'charisma' means.
    Can you think of a famous person today who has 'charisma'?
16. In Judaism Moses is a key figure but there is a strong tendency not to hero-worship him. What do you think are the reasons for this? Do you think there are dangers in hero-worshipping people, if so what are they?

UNIT 2

God's Call

As Moses was brought up as an Egyptian nobleman he never had to work with the other Hebrew people as a slave. However, he grew more and more angry at the way the slaves were being treated. One day, Moses was in the area where the slaves were working and he saw an Egyptian taskmaster beating a slave. Moses became so angry that he hit the taskmaster who fell to the ground and died. The Pharaoh soon found out what had happened and ordered Moses' arrest but Moses was able to escape across the desert.

Moses settled down in the land of Midian. Time passed, Moses married and Zipporah his wife gave birth to a child, but he could not forget what was happening to his people in Egypt. 'They must be saved from slavery,' Moses thought to himself, 'God cannot have deserted them.' Although such thoughts were on his mind, Moses was happy enough to settle down with his wife and family and live a quiet life as a shepherd. Then something changed Moses. Something shook him out of his cosy life and made him attempt what must have seemed the impossible. Moses decided to go back to Egypt and try to free the Hebrew slaves.

What made Moses change so much? What made him decide to take on such a hopeless task? Jewish people believe there is only one possible answer to such questions...all this was the work of God. In the Bible we are told that after a mysterious and frightening experience on a lonely mountain Moses was convinced that God was with him and was directing his life. This extraordinary experience is often simply called 'the Burning Bush' because of the way it is described in the Bible. Out of a bush on fire but undamaged by the flames, we are told, God spoke to Moses and gave him the task of freeing the Hebrew people from slavery.

'And the angel of the Lord appeared to him in a flame of fire out of the midst of a bush; and he looked, and lo, the bush was burning, yet it was not consumed.'
(Exodus, Chapter 3, verse 2.)

Go back to Egypt

Cast: Moses
      Zipporah, Moses' wife
      Jethro, Zipporah's father

Scene: Jethro's house after Moses had come down from the mountain

ZIPPORAH: But why, Moses? I still don't see why you have to go.

MOSES: I can't really explain it myself, Zipporah. I just know it's something I have to do. I've got to go back to Egypt and try to free those slaves.

JETHRO: Moses, tell us again, what happened on the mountain?

MOSES: I was looking after the sheep, but some of them had wandered up the mountain. It was getting late so I climbed the mountain to bring the sheep down for the night.

JETHRO: You shouldn't climb Sinai. I've told you before it belongs to God.

MOSES: I didn't intend going very far. As I came to a clearing something extraordinary happened. There are no words to describe it.

ZIPPORAH: What do you mean? Were you sick? Did you see something?

MOSES: I don't know, Zipporah. I don't understand it myself. It was the place itself. It was so strange. There was something dreadful there. I was terrified but also there was something wonderful. It was so still. Something was there, I could feel it.

JETHRO: Did you see anyone?

MOSES: No . . . there was nothing you could see or touch, but there was something there.

JETHRO: Is it possible, Moses? Has God come to you?

MOSES: It was like being in a different world. As if I had been told, I took off my shoes.

ZIPPORAH: But why did you do that?

JETHRO: The place was holy, Zipporah. You can't stand on holy ground in shoes as if you were just anywhere.

MOSES: And then I knew what God wanted me to do. I have to go back to Egypt.

ZIPPORAH: But how do you know that, Moses? Perhaps you just imagined it all?

MOSES: There's no imagining how I feel now. I just know I have to go. I know God wants me to go and I know somehow God will help me free those slaves. I'm frightened of what might happen but I'm as certain as I'm standing here...I have to go, God has called me.

ZIPPORAH: But it's pointless, Moses. You can't hope to free the slaves. You would need an army.

JETHRO: You're right, Zipporah. On his own he could do nothing but if God has sent him who knows what can be achieved? This is a God with real power. Who knows what God can do? But Moses, you must be certain that this is God's will. It's so easy to fool yourself.

MOSES: Something happened to me on that mountain, Jethro. I don't think I ever really knew God until now. I just can't stay here and pretend nothing has happened. I'll leave for Egypt tomorrow and if God is with me, something, *something* must come of it.

Read the story of the Burning Bush in the Bible, Exodus, Chapters 3–4.

What have you remembered?

1. Why did Moses have to leave Egypt in a hurry?

He was beaten in battle	The slaves were angry with him
He had killed a taskmaster	There was a shortage of food

2. In Midian Moses married and lived as a

merchant	shepherd	fisherman	prince

3. In the Bible we are told that Moses saw the Burning Bush on

Mount Olympus	Mount Tabor	Mount Arafat	Mount Sinai

4. God told Moses that he was to

live a quiet life as a shepherd	lead the people out of slavery
make sure the slaves stayed in Egypt	live all the time on the mountain

Answer the following questions and complete the word puzzle.

5. The Bible tells us that Moses decided to go back to Egypt after seeing a

6. Moses believed He was directing his life

7. Moses took these off because he was on holy ground

8. The Bible tells us the Burning Bush was on fire but it was not

9. Moses felt this when he was called by God

10. Moses also felt this when he was called by God

B						B			
G									
S									
D									
F									
W									

What do you know?

11. In the Bible it is clear that at the Burning Bush Moses did not want to go back to Egypt. Why do you think Moses did not want to return to Egypt? What excuses did he give for not going? (See Exodus, Chapters 3 and 4.)
12. Imagine you also were on Mount Sinai and saw Moses when he believed God spoke to him. Describe what you saw and what happened.
13. When Moses believed that God spoke to him from the Burning Bush he was filled with fear and wonder.
What does 'wonder' mean?
When do you think a person might feel 'wonder'?

What do you think?

14. Moses decided to give up his life in Midian and go back to Egypt. What do you think this tells us about Moses?
15. Can you think of anyone else who changed their life and decided to take on something difficult? Who was he or she and what did they do?
16. In every Jewish synagogue today there is a light which is always kept burning. It is a symbol of the eternal presence of God. Why do you think a light is used as a symbol of God's presence?
17. Apart from the eternal light in a synagogue can you name any other places where eternal lights or flames are used? Why do you think they are used in these places?

UNIT 3

The Fight for Freedom

After Moses' experience on Mount Sinai he returned to Egypt hoping to free the Hebrew slaves. He and his brother Aaron went to the Pharaoh but were unable to persuade him to let the slaves go. The Bible tells us how God caused ten plagues to fall on the Egyptians. Each of these plagues is described in the Bible as a miracle, and many people today believe that all ten took place just as they are described.

Some people have argued that these were not miracles but quite natural disasters. For example, some people have thought that the ninth plague, three days of darkness, was caused by a hot wind from the desert which sometimes blows across Egypt. When it does blow it contains a great amount of sand which darkens the sky for several days. Other people have said that even if all the plagues were natural events, the fact that they all came at the same time was itself miraculous.

1. Nile turns to blood
2. A plague of frogs
3. A plague of gnats
4. A plague of flies
5. A plague on the cattle
6. A plague of boils
7. Hail and thunder
8. A plague of locusts
9. Three days of darkness
10. The death of the first-born

A Jewish family today celebrating the Passover.

Whatever these events were, the Bible makes it clear that up until the ninth plague the Pharaoh was not prepared to give in. It was the tenth plague, which resulted in the death of many young people including the Pharaoh's own son, which finally changed his mind. Some people have suggested that this tenth disaster was a disease, perhaps anthrax. We are told that the Hebrew people were warned of the coming of God's final plague. To protect themselves each family had to sacrifice a lamb and smear some of its blood on the lintel and two door-posts of their house and they were to prepare a special meal. All people inside such houses were to be spared. At midnight God sent the Angel of Death and struck down all the first-born in Egypt, but passed over the houses of the Hebrew slaves. The Pharaoh, filled with grief at the death of so many including his own son, gave Moses permission for the slaves to leave. That night the slaves left Egypt and with Moses leading them they headed out into the desert.

The night of the passing over of the Angel of Death is so important to the Hebrew people that every year since then they have remembered how they gained their freedom. They hold a special festival called 'Pesach'. 'Pesach' means 'the Passover'.

DAILY SCRIBE

PHARAOH SAYS NO!

The Pharaoh was keeping his hardline stand against the demands of the Hebrew slaves, it was reported last night. In spite of intense pressure to give in, the Pharaoh issued a statement saying, 'The slaves will stay and work. I will never free them'. But it also became clear that the slaves were not going to give up their demands. They announced that if they were not released, another disaster would happen in Egypt.

Pharaoh under pressure

MOSES NEW SLAVE LEADER

REPORT EXPLAINS WORST YEAR

Our Science Correspondent
The swarms of insects, the sickness and disease which have swept through the country were due to massive land slides, so says a government report just issued. Government officials have discovered that large quantities of earth have fallen into southern regions of the river Nile. This explains why the river was so muddy red and undrinkable earlier this year.

Breeding-Grounds
The report also says that river sections have become blocked and have developed into main breeding-grounds for thousands of flies, gnats and mosquitoes, and this has

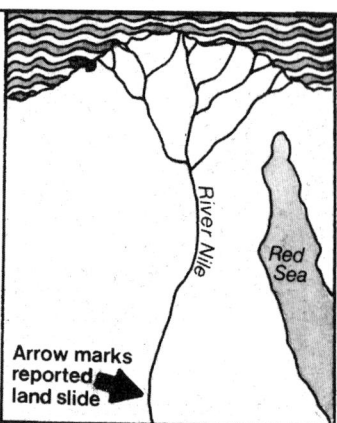

River Nile

Red Sea

Arrow marks reported land slide

been the cause of the vast numbers of frogs which have been such a nuisance in our cities. All this, the report points out, has resulted in a serious threat to public health. Doctors have reported large numbers of people complaining of skin infections and boils. Many farmers have also lost thousands of animals.

Slaves now have to collect their own straw

The Hebrew slaves have a new leader, the ex-prince and nobleman Moses. Their demand that they be freed comes from a small group of slaves, but it has become clear that Moses is their ringleader.

Single-handed
What is Moses like? Undoubtedly he has enormous energy. Virtually single-handed he has raised the Hebrew slaves to action. The man is also no fool. He has spoken directly to the Pharaoh and many report that he speaks with great intelligence and force.

Miracle Worker
Amongst the slaves themselves he has such a reputation that some regard him as a miracle worker. There are rumours that he has predicted recent events in Egypt, like the large numbers of flies, frogs and mosquitoes. It is he more than any other who started the rumours that these events are not just natural disasters but are caused by a god. However, in spite of Moses' ability, he has not found it easy as the leader of these often quarrelsome people.

Straw
Pharaoh's orders that the slaves have to collect their own straw to make bricks brought a storm of protest against Moses. His ability to overcome these protests shows the man's skill and determination. Moses must be watched closely in the next few months. There is little doubt that whatever happens, Moses will be at the heart of it.

HOLIDAY HOMES
by the Great Lake of Fayyum, See Centre Page

WHAT THE *DAILY SCRIBE* SAYS
Does Egypt really need the Hebrew slaves? With their demand this year that they be set free we must seriously ask ourselves, 'Why not let them go?' They are after all the most difficult and troublesome of all of Egypt's work force. These people are proud and independent and make the worst slaves. The taskmasters frequently report surliness and slow work, in spite of the use of the whip. They even stir up trouble amongst other workers. Egypt's economy will not be seriously affected by their loss. We already have a large work force and if necessary this could be increased. The *Daily Scribe* says Egypt can do without these people. They're more trouble than they're worth.

Read the story of the night of the Passover, Exodus, Chapter 12, verses 21–42.

What have you remembered?

Clues Across
1. The fourth plague
2. Which plague ate everything?
4. Moses' brother
5. Some would say, caused by sand from the desert

Clues Down
1. They hopped through the Egyptian homes
3. The darkness lasted this number of days

1. In the Bible story, how many plagues did God cause to fall on the Egyptians?
2. In the Bible story, what was the final plague?
3. What is the name of the Jewish festival which celebrates the night the slaves were freed from Egypt?
4. In the Bible story, what did the Hebrew people do to protect themselves from the final plague?
5. What natural explanation might some people use to account for the ninth plague, the three days of darkness?

What do you know?

6. The report about the Ten Plagues in the newspaper the *Daily Scribe* is the sort of thing an Egyptian might have written. Write a newspaper article about the Ten Plagues which might have been written by a Jew.
7. Write a short play. The scene is Pharaoh's palace just before the tenth plague. Moses and Aaron try to talk Pharaoh into freeing the slaves but Pharaoh refuses. Write down the sort of thing that might have been said.

> *Cast:* Moses
> Aaron
> Pharaoh
> Pharaoh's wife
>
> *Time:* Just before the tenth plague
> *Scene:* Pharaoh's palace

8. One of the traditions of Judaism is that all Jews should try to regard themselves as if they had been freed from slavery in Egypt. In Judaism, Egypt isn't just a place of slavery, it is a symbol of narrowness and of the need to free oneself and to achieve all that one can.
What do you think is meant by a narrow character?
Write a story about a person whose character was narrow.

What do you think?

9. Find out what you can about the Jewish festival of the Passover.
How do Jewish people celebrate this festival today?
Why do you think the festival is so important to the Jewish people?
10. The Ten Plagues are described in the Bible as supernatural miracles.
Do you think the plagues were supernatural miracles? Explain your answer.

The Great Escape

Once Pharaoh said the slaves could go they packed up everything as quickly as possible and left. For over four hundred years the Hebrew people had lived in Egypt and now with Moses at their head they were leaving.

All this was achieved, the Bible tells us, because of God. We are told that God led the way out of Egypt with a pillar of smoke by day and a pillar of fire by night. However, shortly after the slaves had gone Pharaoh changed his mind. He called for his generals and ordered his army of charioteers to bring them back. The Bible then tells us of an extraordinary miracle – the crossing of the Red Sea.

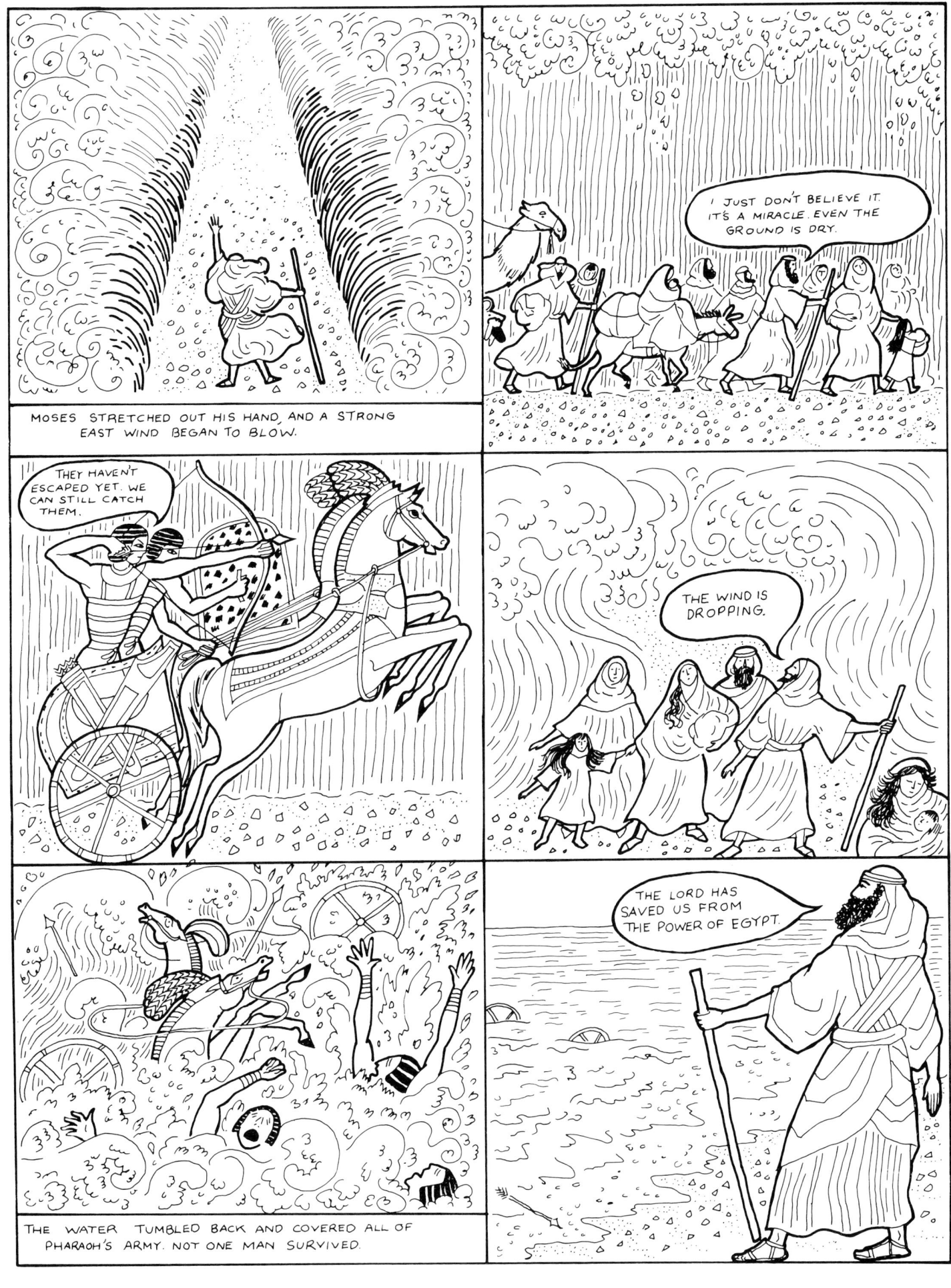

Radio Thebes Broadcasting Company: Radio TBC

Cast: Nefertare: News reader/interviewer
      Memnet: News reporter
        Pepi: Egyptian Field Marshal
    Hunefer: Egyptian High Priest

NEFERTARE:
(News reader)
This is Radio TBC coming to you live. Here are the main news headlines.

The cavalry has failed to bring back the Hebrew slaves. Pharaoh's charioteers made a desperate attempt yesterday to catch up with a large band of escaping slaves. But latest reports reaching us say that the slaves have got away and that some Egyptian soldiers have died. We do not have exact numbers at this stage but for the latest information we go over to our reporter with the forces.

MEMNET:
(Reporter)
I'm standing on the banks of Lake Timsah which was the scene of an extraordinary event last night. This is a vast marshy area. Indeed the local people call it the Sea of Reeds. Yesterday morning it looked as if the Hebrew slaves, who left Egypt several days ago, were trapped. We had reports that Pharaoh's charioteers would be here soon to round up the slaves, but a freak storm blew up and the depth of water of this already shallow area dropped so low that it became possible for the slaves to cross over.

By the time the cavalry arrived the wind was already dropping and it was impossible to continue the chase. Some members of the advance guard were last seen in a particularly dangerous section of boggy marsh land and are now feared dead.

This is Memnet your Radio Thebes reporter returning you now to the studio.

NEFERTARE:
(News reader/ interviewer)
After that report from Memnet we continue the debate about the escape of the slaves. Here in the studio we have a leading military adviser, Field-Marshal Pepi, and also a religious spokesman from the Temple, High Priest Hunefer.

Good evening Field-Marshal. To come straight to the point, the slaves have escaped. Is this a major military blunder?

PEPI:
(Field-Marshal)
A full investigation will of course have to be made but I don't think the army can be blamed. This marshy area is usually impassable but during storms the wind does clear the water and it is possible to cross.

NEFERTARE:
(Interviewer)
But shouldn't this have been realised? Shouldn't the cavalry have got there sooner?

PEPI:
(Field-Marshal)
The problem was known. Weather reports suggested that this could happen and that to prevent the slaves' escape, speed was essential. This was why the chariots were sent and not the usual foot patrol.

NEFERTARE:
(Interviewer) If I can turn now to High Priest Hunefer. The Hebrew people are going to call this a miracle. Is it?

HUNEFER:
(High Priest) Of course not. As Field-Marshal Pepi has explained, this group of people have crossed marshy land. That's hardly a miracle.

NEFERTARE:
(Interviewer) But it's quite a coincidence isn't it? After all, the Hebrew people seem to have been at just the right place at just the right time. Isn't that a miracle?

HUNEFER:
(High Priest) No it's not. I admit these people have been very lucky but surely we're not going to say that every lucky coincidence comes from the gods. People would be announcing miracles every day.

NEFERTARE:
(Interviewer) Well, no doubt the debate will continue but I'm afraid we've run out of time. Thank you gentlemen for being here tonight. We'll be back on the air tomorrow morning with more news and comment but, from all of us here in the studio, good night.

Read the story of crossing of the Red Sea in the Bible, Exodus, Chapter 14, verses 5–30.

What have you remembered?

The Bible says... (Exodus, Chapter 14.)

1. Moses and the Hebrew people crossed the

| Red Sea | River Nile | Dead Sea | River Jordan |

2. By night God led the Hebrew people out of Egypt with a

| Bright star | Pillar of fire | Winged angel | White dove |

3. When the Hebrew people thought they were trapped and were going to be killed many of them

| became angry with Moses | remained calm |
| swam to safety | attacked the Egyptians |

4. When the waters parted the Hebrew people crossed on

| marshy land | boggy land | damp land | dry land |

5. When the waters tumbled back the people who were drowned were the

| Hebrew slaves | Egyptian cavalry | Canaanites | Amorites |

What do you know?

6. For how many years had the Hebrew people lived in Egypt?
7. During the day-time the Bible says God led the way with what?
8. After he had freed the slaves, the Pharaoh changed his mind and decided to do what?
9. In the Bible what happened that caused the sea to divide?
10. After escaping out of Egypt the Bible tells us that Moses led the people into the desert, where God provided them with food. What was the food God provided? (See Exodus, Chapter 16, verses 13–36.)

What do you think?

11. In the radio broadcast how does Memnet explain what happened at the Red Sea? What do you think of this explanation?
12. List some of the main ways in which the radio report differs from the Bible story.
13. Some people have said that over the years the story of what really happened at the Red Sea has become exaggerated. What does 'exaggerated' mean? There are exaggerated stories told about people today. Can you think of an example?
14. Why do you think some stories about people are exaggerated?
15. Why do you think the Hebrew people packed up everything and quickly left Egypt?
16. Try to find out why the Jewish people eat unleavened bread at the Passover (Pesach).
17. A Jewish teacher when asked, 'Do you really believe the Red Sea parted?' shrugged his shoulders and said, 'We escaped.' When he said this what do you think he meant?
18. A Jewish writer once said, 'Whether or not the waters were really divided is not as important as the fact that Moses got the people to move onward. At each step along the way he tried to teach them that in many ways, slavery is easier than freedom.' What do you think was meant by this?
19. Do you think too much importance is often given to the belief in supernatural miracles?

A God of Justice

Having escaped out of Egyptian slavery Moses led the Hebrew people towards Mount Sinai. They headed south deeper and deeper into the desert. The journey was difficult and dangerous and many of the people grumbled and complained. They were short of food and water. An important belief in Judaism is that God was with Moses and the people he was leading. In spite of the difficulties they faced, Moses kept control of the people. As their leader they came to him to sort out their arguments and disputes and Moses began to teach the people to live in peace and harmony. Eventually, with the determined Moses at their head, the Hebrew people arrived at Mount Sinai.

They now had a chance to rest and to think about all that had happened to them. They had suffered a lot together, but in sharing hardship and success they were slowly becoming less like a crowd of people thrown together. More and more, they were becoming a community of people, a nation.

This sense of being a nation was to grow even stronger while the Hebrew people were at Mount Sinai. By far the most important event which was to unite them was their experience of God. In the Bible we are told that Moses gathered all the people around the base of the mountain. From the mountain came smoke, fire and the sound of thunder. What happened next on Sinai was to influence the people deeply. They believed that in a way God appeared to them. Jewish people believe that at Sinai God made them His Chosen People, and a special promise or 'Covenant' was made between God and the people.

'And he gave to Moses, when he had made an end of speaking with him upon Mount Sinai, the two tables of the testimony, tables of stone, written with the finger of God.'
(Exodus, Chapter 31, verse 18.)

The Chosen People were to be those to whom God would give a special way of life. The belief that the Jewish people are God's instrument remains today an important part of Judaism. But although they are 'Chosen', Jews don't believe they are better than any other nation. Jewish people know that like all other people they have many faults, but in spite of their faults they do believe they are the people who were specially chosen to do God's will.

As God's Chosen People, at Sinai the Jews were given God's Law which they were to obey. In the Bible we are told Moses was on the mountain for forty days. According to tradition, while on the mountain God gave Moses two stone tablets on which were inscribed Ten Commandments. These Commandments have become world famous and for many people they are a symbol of law and order, goodness and justice.

The Ten Commandments

1. You shall have no gods before me
2. You shall not make any carved images to worship
3. You shall not misuse God's Name
4. Remember the Sabbath day and keep it holy
5. Honour your father and your mother
6. You shall not kill
7. You shall not commit adultery
8. You shall not steal
9. You shall not lie about your neighbour
10. You shall not covet your neighbour's belongings

According to Jewish tradition Moses was given not only the Ten Commandments but also the first five books of the Bible. In Judaism these five books are called *Torah* which means 'Instruction' or 'Law'. For Jewish people today the Torah is the most important of their holy books.

For Jewish people today the Torah is the most important of their holy books.
It is read every week in all synagogues.

The Law of God

Cast: Moses
       Miriam, Moses' sister
       Benjamin, A Hebrew

Scene: In the camp of the Hebrew people

BENJAMIN: What's so special about these laws anyway? Who needs them?

MIRIAM: We need them. We can't live as a nation without laws.

BENJAMIN: Why not? Everybody knows in their heart you shouldn't steal or kill. Why write it down?

MOSES: Because by writing it down we can be sure everybody knows what they can and can't do. Nobody can then argue and say they didn't know.

BENJAMIN: But some people are still going to steal. Some will even murder. What difference does it make if you write a law saying they shouldn't?

MOSES: It makes a lot of difference. Suppose Miriam here stole one of your goats. What would you do?

BENJAMIN: I would do what everybody else would do. I would take it back.

MIRIAM: But I could ask some of my friends to help me. If they catch you, they will fight you off.

BENJAMIN: Well then I would get some friends. Joel and Zadok would help me.

MIRIAM: But don't you see what would happen? There would be a fight. Someone could get hurt and so a theft which should be easily sorted out could become very serious.

MOSES: All that happens in the end is that the biggest and strongest, or those with most friends, end up winning. Where's the justice in that?

BENJAMIN: I still don't see what difference a law will make.

MOSES: On its own not a lot but we will have a system to make the law work. If Miriam steals one of your goats you don't try to steal it back. You go to the judges I have named. One of them will listen to the evidence and if you're right you will get your goat back and Miriam will be punished.

MIRIAM: Don't you see? Without a law we live like animals, always fighting for what we want. With a law we have justice and fairness.

BENJAMIN: It will never work.

MIRIAM: God will make it work.

MOSES: The God that helped us escape from Egypt is a God of justice. That is why we were given just laws. With such laws no one need be a slave and no one need live in fear.

MIRIAM: Come on...let's not talk any more about stealing and fighting. In (To Benjamin) years to come people will take laws and judges and courts for granted. They will forget that we often made life for each other uncertain and evil.

MOSES: She's right Benjamin. People will forget how we worshipped evil gods with evil sacrifices. We have a holy God and with the help of God's law we must try to be a holy nation.

Read the story of the giving of the Ten Commandments in the Bible, Exodus, Chapters 19–20.

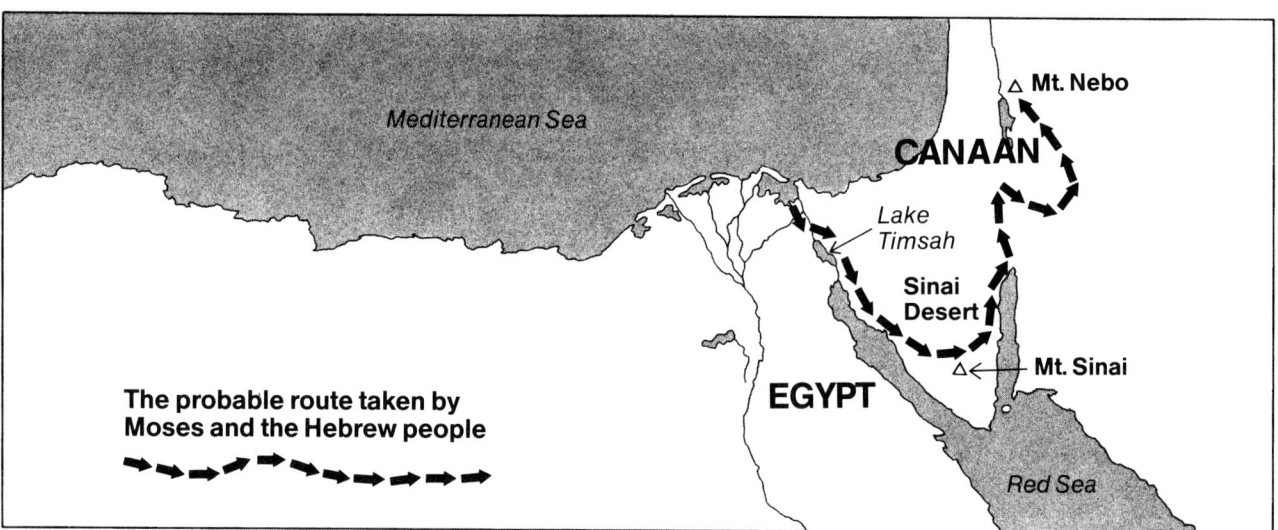

What have you remembered?

Complete the sentences. Match the phrases in the left-hand column with the phrases from the right.

1. From Mount Sinai there came smoke,	Chosen People
2. God gave to Moses two tablets of stone on which was written	Torah
3. The first five books of the Bible in Hebrew are called	five books of the Bible
4. Jewish people believe they are God's	God appeared to them
5. At Mount Sinai Jewish people believe that in a way	fire and the sound of thunder
6. As well as the Ten Commandments God gave Moses the first	the Ten Commandments

7. What is the Hebrew word for the first five books of the Bible?

| Torah | Talmud | Ten Commandments | Testament |

8. For how many days was Moses on Mount Sinai?

| 3 days | 10 days | 30 days | 40 days |

9. Sharing hardship and success together helped to form the Hebrew people

| into a crowd | into a nation | into slaves | into a lawless mob |

10. Moses taught that there was a God of

| violence | thunder | justice | mountains |

What do you know?

11. Write a short story showing what could happen if there were no laws, judges or courts.
12. The fourth Commandment is, 'Remember the Sabbath day to keep it holy'. What do Jewish people do on the Sabbath?
13. Why is the Sabbath day so important for the Jewish people?
14. While on the journey to Mount Sinai what advice did Moses' father-in-law, Jethro, give to Moses? (See Exodus, Chapter 18, verses 13–27.)
15. What was the Promise made between God and the Jewish people?
16. Describe what Moses did to seal the Promise or Covenant made between God and the people. (See Exodus, Chapter 24, verses 1–11.)

What do you think?

17. In the desert Moses proved himself to be a great leader.
    What sort of person do you think makes a good leader?
18. What sort of problems did Moses have to deal with when he and the Hebrew people were in the desert?
    What do you think made Moses a good leader?
19. Why do you think Moses and his friends believed God was with them in the desert, helping them?
20. Why do you think the Ten Commandments are thought by many people to be so important?
21. What do you think are the advantages in having clear laws?

The Desert Ordeal

For forty days Moses was on Sinai while the people waited for him at the base of the mountain. In spite of all that had happened, without Moses the people soon lost their faith in God. They made themselves a Golden Calf god and they began to sing and dance around it. While all this was going on Moses came down from the mountain. He was horrified to discover that the people had broken their promise to worship God only. Eventually however, God forgave them, and repeated the promise to make them the Chosen People. The promise was sealed with a special ceremony at which Moses repeated all of God's words and the people solemnly promised to keep all the Commandments.

All of the Laws were then put inside a wooden box which was called the Ark and this was then placed inside a special tent called the Tabernacle. With several men carrying the Ark in front of them, the Hebrew people left Mount Sinai but God had said that they were not ready to enter the Promised Land. For forty years they were to wander in the desert. All this time Moses carefully taught the people God's Law. They had to fight several battles against various tribes and kingdoms but finally Moses led them towards the Promised Land. However, Moses himself did not enter this land with his people. From a mountain called Nebo he looked out and saw the land promised to his people. Then, his task at last completed, he died.

'And now, O Israel, give heed to
the statutes and the ordinances which
I teach you, and do them, that
you may live, and go in and take
possession of the land which the
Lord the God of your fathers, gives you.'
(Deuteronomy, Chapter 4, verse 1.)

MOSES IS DEAD

The Hebrew people on the move

Moses, the unchallenged leader of the Hebrew people for over forty years, died yesterday. Today all the Hebrew people are mourning. Over the years this man has become a legend in his own lifetime. Stories are told of how he appeared in Egypt apparently from nowhere.

Slaves

There it is known he assumed leadership of a group of slaves. From under the nose of Pharaoh and his army Moses led those slaves into the desert and freedom. It was while they were in the desert that Moses was able to organise and discipline these people.

Laws

He wrote a system of laws which his own people regard as having come from a god. So important are these laws to these people that violence and disputes amongst them are not serious problems. Moses has died but in his own lifetime he had made these people a real force in the area. In battle they can challenge anyone. Today they stand ready to attack Canaan. According to reports Moses died on Mount Nebo looking at Canaan and telling his people that this was the Promised Land which was to be theirs.

MOSES...a legend

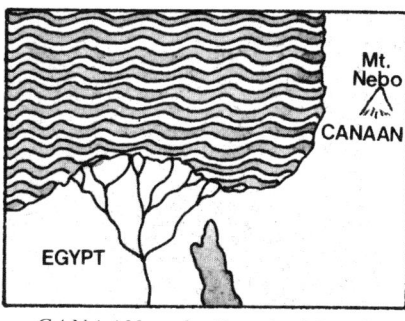

CANAAN...the Promised Land?

Amalekite Star Exclusive
JOSHUA TO BE NEW LEADER

Joshua the son of Nun is the new leader of the Hebrew people. With the death of Moses, once again the Hebrew people have shown their unity as a nation. Instead of a struggle for power, Joshua, Moses' right-hand man for many years, has become the new leader.

Joshua has a reputation as a skilful army commander. It was he who led the Hebrew people in their defeat of the Amorites and of the King of Bashan.

Spies

Already it is claimed that Hebrew spies have reported back to Joshua and that he plans next to capture the rich land of Canaan.

Joshua ... new leader

MOSES, THE MAN I KNEW

Amalekite Star Special Correspondent

Moses was a great political leader but he was also a great religious leader. I for one would say that Moses' religious ideas will influence people for a long time to come.

A GOD OF EVERYTHING

Whenever I met Moses, as I did on several occasions, I was struck by the man's modesty. Others have remarked on his determination but of all his qualities I was impressed by his modesty. Everything he achieved, he said, was due to God. For Moses there was only one God but his God was more than just a God of wind or thunder. The God Moses worshipped was a God of everything. Moses refused to allow statues or paintings to be made of God.

HOLY GOD

God was too great, too holy to be painted. Moses also said that God wanted people to act fairly. God was to be worshipped by obeying God's laws not by superstitious rituals or cruel sacrifices. Who knows what will happen to these extraordinary ideas? Will they survive or be forgotten? However, one thing is certain, a great man has died and wherever people love justice and fairness, Moses' name will be remembered.

Read the story of the death of Moses, Deuteronomy, Chapter 34, Verses 1–12.

What have you remembered?

Complete the sentences. Match the phrases in the left-hand column with phrases from the right.

1.	While Moses was on Mount Sinai the people made	to keep all the Commandments
2.	Moses repeated all of God's words and the people promised	special tent called the Tabernacle
3.	All of the laws were put inside the Ark and the Ark was placed inside a	he did not enter it
4.	All the time the Hebrew people were in the wilderness Moses carefully	a Golden Calf
5.	From Mount Nebo Moses could see the Promised Land but	taught them God's law

What do you know?

6. What did the people do when they had made the Golden Calf?
7. After Moses came down from the mountain what did the Hebrew people solemnly promise?
8. What was the wooden box called in which the laws were kept?
9. For how many years did Moses and the Hebrew people wander in the desert?
10. What did Moses see from the top of Mount Nebo?
11. When Moses realised he was dying who did he make the new leader?
12. On the top of what mountain did Moses die?
13. What was the name of the special tent in which the Ark was placed?
14. When the people made the Golden Calf which of the Ten Commandments did they break?
15. An idol can be a stone or a wooden statue which is believed to be a god. Or it could be anything (other than God) which takes over a person's life. An idol is something which is not worth worshipping. Make a list of things which can seem to take over a person's life, i.e., drugs, fame. Write a story about a person whose life is taken over by one of the things on your list. Explain in your story what happens to this person.

What do you think?

16. In the newspaper, the *Amalekite Star*, one of the writers tries to sum up Moses' life. Write a report of your own in which you sum up what you think Moses was like and what you think Moses achieved.

17. In the Bible we are told the Hebrew people were not ready to enter the Promised Land but would have to spend many years in the wilderness. Moses used that time to do what?
    In what way do you think the Hebrew people changed in that time?

18. Every year the Jewish people celebrate a festival called Sukkot (Tabernacles) which remembers the time when they wandered through the desert for forty years. How do Jewish people today celebrate Sukkot? Why do you think Jewish people regard the forty years in the desert as being so important that they wish every year to be reminded of it?

19. After all that he had achieved, Moses saw the Promised Land but he was not allowed to enter it. What lesson do you think a member of Judaism might draw from the way Moses died?

20. One Jewish writer said the festival of Shavuot celebrates, 'the greatest epiphany in the history of the cosmos: God revealing Himself directly to 600 000 people.'
    What is an epiphany?
    What is the cosmos?
    What does Shavuot celebrate?
    How is this festival celebrated?

'On the first day of the first month you shall erect the tabernacle of the tent of meeting. And you shall put in it the ark of the testimony . . .'
(Exodus, Chapter 40, verses 2–3.)

Lawgiver, Prophet, Teacher

The journey out of Egypt and the revelation at Mount Sinai are of central importance in the religion of Judaism. For Jewish people Moses is a key figure and is seen as the great example of a prophet and messenger of God's word. The Bible says of him, 'And there has not arisen a prophet in Israel like Moses, whom the Lord knew face to face.' (Deuteronomy, Chapter 34, verse 11.)

Jewish people believe that on Mount Sinai Moses was given the Torah, the unique revelation of God's law. However, Moses was not only given the written law on Sinai. God also spoke to him, explaining the meaning and purpose of the law. In Judaism, it is believed Moses taught the Jewish people the written law (the Torah) and also what God had spoken to him (the oral law). For this reason the great Rabbis and teachers of Judaism regard themselves as receivers of the oral law from Moses. It is this oral law which forms the foundation of the Talmud, which is a vast collection of discussions and comments of many great Rabbis. This is why Moses is regarded as the greatest teacher and is often called 'Mosheh Rabbenu' which means Moses our Rabbi (teacher).

However, Jews do not regard Moses as perfect, or without fault. It has been said that he was hot-tempered, cold towards his wife and family and that he argued with God. In Judaism, there is no doubt that Moses is seen as human, with human faults. As one Rabbi said, 'Moses has no role in heaven. He does not sit at God's right hand to relay the prayers of the faithful.' It is significant that of all the great leaders of religion Moses is the only one with no shrine dedicated to him.

Nevertheless, it remains true that the Jewish people regard Moses as the faithful servant of God and as the great leader. His courage, faith, determination and sense of justice remain an example to everyone. In the Talmud it is written that at his death:

'The heavens wept and exclaimed, "The pious one hath departed, there is none upright among men."'

'When Joshua searched for his friend and teacher and failed to find him, he wept bitterly and cried, "Help me, O Lord, for the pious have ceased to be!" The angels proclaimed, "He executed the justice of the Lord"; and Israel added, "And His judgments with Israel." And together they exclaimed, "He shall come in peace; they shall rest in their beds, every one walking in his uprightness." Blessed be the memory of the just.'